Grand1 Thomas Jackson's Victorian Cures and Recipes

Illustrations by Maltings Partnership
© 1985.
First published - ISBN 0-946404-60-7
This edition - ISBN 1-903627-27-3 - July 2002

2002

My Derbyshire History Series

Walk & Write Ltd.

*Unit 1, Molyneux Business park, Whitworth Road,
Darley dale, Matlock, Derbyshire. DE4 2HJ
Tel/fax - 01629-735911
email - marathonhiker@aol.com*

'Half a pound of two-penny rice,
Half a pound of treacle;
Mix it up and make it nice,
Pop goes the weasel'.

INTRODUCTION

Thomas Jackson was born in Belper in 1854, becoming a Master Painter and Decorator, and eventually employing 25 tradesmen at his buisness in Ray Street. During his apprenticship he walked to Heanor and back each day. He methodically and neatly wrote down each cure or advice in a journal, which can be clearly read today. He wrote for the local papers and hoped to write a novel. His mother was a Hudson, whose relatives were the famous Hudson Bay Company. He married a Heanor women and had eight children, but only two daughters and four sons survived infancy. He died in Heanor in 1921.

He was a deeply religious man and founded a Sunday School for deprived children. His own children went to Sunday School and each Sunday a poor child was given lunch at his house.

This book is a small part of a larger collection of "cures" and recipes, collected by Thomas Jackson, at a time when such knowledge was an essential part of everyday life. Today we visit our doctor for advice and a prescription, but in Victorian Times, they had to rely on home made cures, concocted from domestic ingredients, supplemented by herbs gathered at the wayside and brought from the herbalist. Such would require collecting and preserving, and this would require considerable knowledge. The recipes and cures are taken from the original journal, loaned by his grandaughter, Mrs. Anne Jessica Williamson.

Please note - some of the cures are marked with a skull and crossbones, indicating they are dangerous and possibly lethal.

16

Preserved Peel Make a thick syrup of white sugar, chop
the lemon fine and boil in the syrup 10 mins
put in jars and gum over.

17

Chutney 8 oz apples, 8 oz tomatoes, salt, brown sugar,
2 oz ginger, 2 oz garlic, 3 qts shalots, 1 qt vinegar,
juice of 1 lemon, mix well, put into covered
jar, keep in warm place, stir every day for
a month then strain and bottle.

18

Banbury Cakes. 1ᵒᶻ Currants, ¼ᵒᶻ Beef suet, 3 oz mixed peel
shred into small pieces ½ oz mixed spice
¼ᵒᶻ pounded ratafias, make a light paste
roll thin spread over it a mixture of spices,
put thin top on mark into divisions bake
in quick oven divide when warm and
dust with powdered lump sugar.

Extract from the original recipe and remedy book

For a Cold   Boil a tablespoonful of flaxseed in 1pt. of water and pour over a lemon (sliced thinly) and drink as hot as possible just before going to bed.

Editor's note: Flaxseed is better known today as Linseed.

Reserved Peel   Make a thick syrup of white sugar, chop the lemon fine and boil in the syrup 10 minutes. Put in jars and gum over.

Chutney   8oz. apples, 8oz. tomatoes, salt, brown sugar, 2oz. ginger, 2oz. garlic, 3qts. shalots, 1qt. vinegar, juice of 1 lemon, mix well and put into covered jar. Keep in warm place and stir every day for a month, then strain and bottle.

Banbury Cakes   1lb. currants, ¼lb. beef suet, 3oz. mixed peel. (shred into small pieces), ¼oz. mixed spice, ¼lb. pounded ratafias₁, make a light paste roll it thin. Spread over it a mixture of spices, put thin top on mark into divisions. Bake in quick oven divide when warm and dust with powdered lump sugar.

Bury Simnel Cakes   3lbs. flour, ½lb. butter (rub into flour), 3lbs. currants, 1 lb. raisins, 2oz. peel (shred fine), 1oz. each of sweet and bitter almonds (blanched and chopped fine), ¾lb. sugar, 6 eggs, ½oz. volatile ammonia₂, ¼oz. yeast, mix well with ½pt. cream. Make into cakes, prove and bake in quick oven.

Sponge Cakes   8 eggs, 1lb. lump sugar, ¾lb. flour, rind of lemon (grated), ½ a nutmeg. Beat the eggs for 10 minutes, add sugar, peel and nutmeg, beat again for 10 minutes. Add flour, mix and pour into tins and bake in quick oven.

Ginger Beer   1lb. lump sugar, 1oz. crushed ginger, ¾oz. cream of tartar, 2 sliced lemons, 1 gallon boiling water, when lukewarm add 1½oz. yeast.

Healing Salve   1oz. mutton suet, 1oz. resin, ½oz. best olive oil.

Cough Mixture   1 handful of horehound₃, sprig of wormwood, add 1qt. water boiled down to 1pt., 4oz. lump sugar, 4oz. honey, 1oz. spanish juice, 1oz. sugar candy, ½ teacupful of raspberry vinegar.

Kitchen Spice   2oz. black pepper, 1oz. ginger, 8oz. of cinnamon allspice, 8oz. nutmeg, 1oz. cloves and 6ozs. dry salt. Use for soups, gravies etc.

To Dust Steel   Dip a brush in paraffin then into emery powder, brush the steel and polish with clean leather.

Gingerbread   ½lb. sugar, ¼lb. butter, ¼oz. soda, ¼oz. ginger, cup of milk, sufficient flour to roll thin into sheets.

Table Beer   5 gallon water, 1lb. linseed, 2oz. gentian, 2oz. spanish juice, 2oz. coriander seeds, 2oz. sugar, 2oz. liquorice.

Ginger Wine   20lbs. sugar (dissolve in 9½ gallons of boiling water), 12oz. bruised ginger. Boil for ¼ hour, when nearly cold add ½pt. yeast, pour into cask to ferment taking care to fill the cask from time to time with the surplus of the liquor made for that purpose. When fermentation ceases rack off the wine and bottle when transparent. To flavour, boil rind of lemon to ginger.

Lemon Cheese Cakes   1lb. sugar, 2oz. butter, 4 eggs, 30 drops essence of lemon, ¼ teaspoonful tart$_4$ acid, 1 tablespoonful of water. Ready for use when well mixed.

Scones   1lb. flour, 2lbs. butter, 2 teaspoonfuls of baking powder, ½ teaspoonful of salt, ½pt. milk, 1 teaspoonful of sugar, rub butter in mix light. Roll thin and bake in quick oven.

Ginger Bread   ¾lb. treacle, ½lb. sugar, 6oz. butter, melt and pour on 12oz. flour, a teaspoonful of ground ginger and allspice and the grated rind of a lemon. Bake in shallow tins.

Sore Throat   Steep sage leaves in vinegar and inhale the steam through a funnel.

Omelet A la Cheshire   Mix 2 eggs with 2oz. of flour, add pinch of salt, 2oz. fine sugar, ½pt. milk, dissolve 1oz. butter in a hot frying pan, pour in 2 tablespoonfuls of the batter and let it spread all over the pan. When firm put a teaspoonful of jam and a dessertspoonful of rich custard in the middle of the omelet. Fold it over and roll it round and round. Arrange neatly on hot dish, sift sugar over them and serve immediately. They are sometimes made with beaten egg and sugar only.

Cake   A cupful of sugar, 1lb. butter, 1pt. milk, 2oz. currants, teaspoonful cream of tartar, put into the flour ½ teaspoonful of carb soda$_5$ dissolved in the milk and enough to make stiff batter.

Currant Bread   2oz. cream tartar, 1lb. flour, rub into it 4oz. butter, 8oz. currants, 6oz. sugar, 1pt. milk, 1oz. carb soda (dissolved), little spice and salt to taste, 2 eggs. (4oz. of citron$_6$ will improve it).

Flat Irons   If rough rub them, then rub on fine salt.

Potato Bread   5lbs. flour, 2lbs. potatoes. Boil and strain. Yeast as usual.

To Test
Velvet   Obtain a sample and crease it by pressing a sharp edged paper knife against the pile, if the pile does not come up again after the pressure is removed it certainly will not resist that which comes with even the most careful useage.

Oatmeal Pudding

Soak ½pt. fine oatmeal for 12 hours. Pour 1pt boiling water or milk over it. Add salt and put into buttered basin just large enough to hold it with a well floured cloth tied lightly over it, boil for 1½ hours. Turn it out and serve with cream or thickened flour.

Sherbert Powder

½lb. lump sugar, ¼lb. tart[4] acid, ¼lb. carb soda[5] , 50 drops of essence of lemon.

Luncheon Cake

12oz. flour, ¼lb. butter, ¼lb. sugar, ¼lb. currants, 3 eggs, 2oz peel, a little grated nutmeg, ginger and allspice, a very little salt, rub the butter into flour then add other ingredients plus one teaspoonful of baking powder.

Ginger Nuts

1lb. flour, 1lb. treacle, 3oz. fudge, ¼lb. butter, 1½oz. ground ginger, 3oz. each of citron[6] and peel (cut small), mix well and lay by till morning. Make into cakes and bake in quick oven.

Ginger Wine

10pts. water, when boiling add ½lb. ginger and boil until reduced to 7pts. Take off, strain on 6lbs. course sugar, put again on the fire with the whites of 5 eggs beat up very light and let all boil together, well. Add 1pt. water and when the eggs come to the top, skim off and let it stand for 24 hours to cool then add the juice of 12 lemons and 6 oranges with half of the rind cut and 3 drops of cinnamon. Make up to 10pts. with cold boiled water.

A Nice Dish

2 eggs, 1pt. milk, cut bread in slices, dip the bread in batter and fry each side brown in butter, then boil 1 cup of sugar in 2 cups of water, flavour with lemon then pour over bread and cover dish so as to steam and keep hot, reserve part of sauce to put on each slice when serving.

Lemon Marmalade

Squeeze the lemons, boil the rind in water till soft then take out the pith and pound the remainder till fine, mixing with it a little of the juice, pass all with the remainder of the juice through a sieve into a preserving pan, add ¾lb. lump sugar to every pound of pulp. Boil ½ hour or more till it sets when cold into jelly.

Chocolate Jumbles

1 cupful of butter, 2 cupfuls of sugar, 3oz flour, 2oz. grated chocolate, 4 eggs, 1 teaspoonful carb soda[5] and cream of tartar, a little salt. Roll thin and bake in quick oven.

Chapped Hands

¾ glaziers putty[9], 1oz. camphorated oil, 1oz. glycerine, 1oz. castor oil, mix well, if too soft thicken with flour.

Nerve **Tonic** [18]	2drms. extract of scullcap, 2drms. extract of chamomile, 1drm. extract of boneset, 1 scruple pulverised cayenne, 1drm. of quinine, ½drm. oil of Valerian. Beat well together and make 90 pills. Dose for an adult 1 every 2 or 3 hours.
Stomachic **Bitters** [19]	2oz. gentian root, 10oz. dried orange peel, ½oz. Cardamon (all bruised), 1qt. whisky. Let it stand for 2 weeks. Use for dyspepsia, loss of appetite and general weakness etc. Dose: one or two tablespoonsful in water 3 times a day.
Curry Meat	Cut fresh meat from the bones allowing to every pound of meal a dessertspoon of curry powder. Dip the meat into the powder. Slice some onions quite thin, put some butter into a frying pan, fry the meat and onions till a nice brown. Drain them from the fat and put them into a saucepan with a little salt. The bones should be made into a gravy and poured boiling on the meat which must simmer gently for 1 hour. Mix a little flour with the rest of the curry powder and some cold water to a thick paste, add gradually a little of the gravy and pour it on the meat. Give all a good stir and let it boil for 10 minutes giving it an occassional shake. Serve in dish with a border of boiled rice around it.
Lotion for **Gums**	20 drops carbolic acid[10], 2 drms. spirits of wine, 6oz. distilled water, use first a soft tooth brush slightly dampened with water, then a second slightly dampened with a little lotion. After using this for a short time the gums become less tender and the impurity of the breath is removed.
Tapioca **Cream**	Soak a tablespoonful of tapioca over night in enough water to cover it and add to this 3oz. sugar, the yolk of 2 eggs and a little nutmeg. Beat well together. Boil 1 qt. milk, stir in the mixture and cook for 5 or 10 minutes. Pour into serving dish and spread over top the white of the eggs beaten to a stiff froth with 2oz. of sugar and a small teaspoonful of vanilla. Set in the oven to brown slightly. Eat cold.
Watery **Potatoes**	Put a piece of lime as large as an egg in the water the potatoes are to be boiled in.
Lemon Syrup	1 dozen lemons. Press the juice into a bowl, remove all seeds and all pulp from rind and boil in 1pt. of water for a few minutes, then strain the water with the juice, add 1lb. sugar, boil for ten minutes then bottle.
Ginger Snaps	1 cupful of brown sugar, 1 of treacle, 1 of melted lard, 2 tablespoonsful of ground alum[11], dissolved in 4 teas-poonsful of water, 5 teaspoonsful of soda dissolved in ½ cup of boiling water, 2 tablespoonsful of ginger.

An Expectorant	For asthma and cough to promote expectoration and remove tightness of the chest, the following is a valuable compound. 1oz. extract of cabbage[12], 1oz. lobelia, 1oz. blood root, 1oz. pleurisy root, 1oz. ginger, 1pt. water, 3 pts. alcohol. Dose 1 to 4 teaspoonsful.
Anti-Billious Pills [14]	5oz. pulverised aloes, ¼drm. carbolic soap, 1oz. gamboge, 1oz. colocynth, 1oz. extract gentian, 1oz. mandrake, 2oz. cayenne, ½drm. oil of peppermint. Mix well and form into 3 grain pills. Dose 3 to 5.
Rheumatic Tincture	1½oz. peppermint water, ½oz. wine of colchicum[15] root, 1 grain sulphate of morphine, 1 scruple magnesia. 1 teaspoonful 3 times a day or 4 times if very bad.
Bronchitis [16]	3 grains tasmin, 3-4 parts of grain of extract of belladonna, 2½ grains of extract of colchicum, 3oz. infusion of senna, 1½oz. fennel water, 1½oz. syrup of marshmallow. Mix well. A tablespoonful to be taken every 2 hours if chronic.
Compound Spirits of Lavender [17]	2drms. dried lavender flowers, 2drms. nutmeg, 2drms. mace, 2drms. cloves, 2oz. cinnamon. Pulverise these and add 1qt. of spirits, let it then stand for a week and then strain off the liquid. Dose: one or two tablespoonsful may be taken often in a little water with lump sugar. Useful in all nervous affections.
Cough	½oz. tincture lobelia, 2oz. tincture of blood root, ½drm. oil of spearmint, 5oz. treacle. Dose: ½ teaspoonful as often as needed.
Chilblains [20]	1drm. sulphuric acid, 1drm. turpentine, 3drms. oil of cloves. Mix the oil and turps first then gradually add the sulphuric acid. To be rubbed on two or three times a day.
Sleeplessness	1 grain camphor formed inro a pill followed by a draught of 1½oz. of the infusion of hops with 5 drops of sulphuric ether[21].
Bowel Complaint	1oz. powdered rhubarb, 1 teaspoonful pearlash[22]. When cold add one tablespoonful of essence of peppermint. Dose: 2 tablespoonfuls 3 times a day.
Diarrhoea [24]	1oz. syrup of orange peel, 2 grains acitate of morphine, 6drms. tincture of cinnamon, 2drms. tincture of cardamon. Mix. Dose: 1 teaspoonful 3 times a day.

Toothache

7

10 drops spirit of camphor, 10 drops oil of cloves, 15 drops chloroform, 15 drops spirit of ether. Apply to the cavity or rub the gum a little.

Chilblains	2qts. lard, 1pt. turpentine, ¼pt. camphor. Rub into parts affected. It is a capital remedy.
Stomach Pills 26	8 grains pulverised rhubarb and guaiacum, 2 grains galbanum and ipecacuanha. Mix and make 8 pills. Dose: 1 or 2 pills night and morning. Use for weak stomach and billious condition.
Stomach Pill	1drm. powdered cayenne pepper, 2drms. rhubarb. Make into a mass with syrup and divide into 60 pills. Dose: 2 every day an hour before dinner.
Spiced Bitters 27	10 tubs poplar bark, 2 tubs cayberry bark, 2 tubs calmony bark, 1 tub golden seal, 1 tub cloves, ½ tub cayenne pepper, 16 tubs loaf sugar. Pulverise and mix well. Dose: put a tablespoonful of the mixture with 4oz. sugar into a qt. of boiling water. Take a wineglass 3 times a day before eating.
Cough Mixture 28	1oz. syrup of tolu, ½oz. syrup of squills, 2drms. wine of ipecacuanha, 5drms. paregoric, 1½oz. gum acacia mucilage. Mix well. Dose: 1 teaspoonful occasionally.
Cough Syrup 29	4 grains acetate of morphine, 2 drms. tincture of blood root, 3drms. antimonial wine, 3drms ipecacuanha wine, 3oz. wild cherry. Dose: 1 teaspoonful 2 or 3 times a day.
Poultice for a Fester	Boil bread in the settlings of strong beer. Apply the poultice in the usual manner. This has saved many an hour of suffering.
Toothache	1 scruple each of gum opium, gum camphor, turpentine. Rub in a mortar to a paste, put it in the hollow tooth. This will cure and ever prevent the toothache.
Stings	Bind on the place a thick plaster of common salt or pearlash, moistened. It will soon extract the venom.
Itch Ointment 32	2oz. sublimed sulphur, 1oz. sub-carbonate of potash, 8oz. lard. Mix well and apply freely.
For the Teeth	Make charcoal of bread, pulverise it until it is reduced to an impalpable powder, then apply daily morning and night with a soft brush and cold water. This will keep the teeth white and cure diseases of the gums.

13

Charcoal and its Uses

Charcoal laid flat while cold on a burn will cause the pain to abate. Tainted meat surrounded with it is sweetened. Strewn on heaps of decomposed peels, or over dead animals it prevents unpleasant odours. Foul water is purified by it. It sweetens offensive air if placed in shallow trays around apartments. It is so porous that it absorbs and condenses gases most rapidly. It makes an unrivalled poultice for malignant wounds and sores. In all cases of proud flesh[8] it is invaluable. It hurts no texture injuries, no colour, a simple disinfectant.

Tapeworm [33]

2 scruples of solid extract of malefern, 14 grains gamboge, 18 grains scammony. Mix and divide into 20 pieces. Dose: 2 pills morning and night.

Diarrhoea

2drms. fluid extract of colombo[34], 2drms. fluid extract of rhubarb, 1drm. fluid extract of ginger, 1qt. water. Mix. Dose: 1drm. every one or two hours.

Chalk Mixture

½oz. prepared chalk, 2drms. sugar, 2drms powdered gum arabic, 4 fluid drms. each of cinnamon water and water. Rub together till thoroughly mixed. Dose: 1 teaspoonful often repeated. This is valuable for acidity of stomach.

Whooping Cough	1oz. powdered alum, 1pt. water. Heat the water till the alum is dissolved, add 1 tub best sugar and simmer until a syrup is formed, then strain and when cold use. Dose: from 1 to 2 teaspoonsful a day.
Tealers Powder	1½drms. tart soda, 1½ scruples carb soda, 35 grains tart acid. Mix, then put in 1pt. water.
Wash for Sore Mouth 36	2oz. fluid extract of cranesbill, 2oz. fluid extract of black cohosh, 2oz. fluid extract of golden seal, 2oz. fluid extract of witch hazel, 4qts. of water. Use as a wash as often as may be required.
Fragrant Breath	1 gill sherry wine, 1drm. ground cloves, ¼oz. bruised caraway seeds. Put them all together in an ½pt. bottle and let them stand for several days shaking the bottle every morning and night. Strain the tincture through linen then add 5 drops oils of roses or 10 drops of lavender. A few drops on a lump of sugar will secure a breath of flowers.
Isinglass Jelly	2oz. isinglass, 1qt. water, boil to 1pt., strain and add 1pt. milk and 1oz. white sugar. This is excellent for persons recovering from sickness and for children who have bowel complaints.
Cancer 37	Take equal parts of fresh poke weed, yellow dock, and blood root. Evaporate the juice by the means of a sand bath, to the consistency of tar. The ointment should be applied after the cuticle has been removed by a blister a day. The parts should be washed with French brandy after each application.
Irish Moss Jelly	½oz. Irish moss, ½pt. fresh milk. Boil down to a pint, strain and add sugar and lemon juice sufficient to give it an agreeable flavour.
Tapioca Jelly	Tapioca 2 large tablespoonsful, 1pt. water, boil gently for 1 hour or until it appears like a jelly, then add sugar, nutmeg, with lemon juice to flavour.
Rice Jelly	Mix ¼oz. of rice picked and washed with ½oz. loaf sugar and just sufficient water to cover it. Boil until it assumes a jelly like appearance, strain and season to suit taste.
Bread Jelly	Boil 1qt. of water and let it cool. Take one third of a loaf of bread, slice it, pare of the crust, and toast it to a light brown, put it in the water in a covered vessel and boil gently till you find on putting some in a spoon to cool it has become jelly, strain and cool. When used warm a cupful sweeten with sugar and add a little grated lemon peel.

Sick Headache

13

Fluid extract of ladies slipper, ½oz., fluid extract of catnip, ½oz., fluid extract of scullcap, ½oz. 1pt., water. Dose 1 to 3 tablespoonsful.

Restorative Jelly

Take a leg of well fed pork, beat it and break the bone, put it in 3 galls. of water and let it simmer to one. Stew ½oz. each of mace and nutmeg in it, strain through a fine sieve. When cold take off the fat, give a coffee cup full morning, noon, and night, adding salt to taste.

To Clean Brushes

A few drops of liquid ammonia in basin of water, soak brushes for two minutes.

Calves Foot Jelly

Boil 2 calves feet in 1 gall. of water till reduced to 1qt. Strain and when cool, skim carefully, add the white of six eggs well beaten to a pt. of wine, ½lb. loaf sugar, and the juice of 4 lemons. Mix them well, boil for a few minutes stirring constantly, and pass through a flannel strainer. In some cases the wine should be omitted.

Slippery Elm Jelly

Take of the flowers of slippery elm 2 teaspoonsful, 1pt. cold water, simmer until it becomes a jelly, sweeten with honey. This is excellent for all diseases of the throat, lungs, coughs, colds, bronchitis, inflamation of the lungs etc.

Maids of Honour Cakes

Beat 1lb. loaf sugar with the yolk of 12 eggs in a mortar, 1oz. blanched almonds sweet and 12 bitter and 4 tablespoonsful of orange water. The almonds to be mixed last, line patty pans with good puff paste and fill with mixture. Bake in a moderate oven.

Nutritive Fluids No. 1

Put 1pt. new milk and 1qt. soft water in a vessel over a low fire. rub 2 teaspoonsful of flour, 2 of carbonate of magnesia together with a little milk into a soft batter free from lumps, add this to the milk and water, as soon as they begin to boil. Boil gently for 5 mins. no longer stirring constantly. Pour into an earthen or glass dish to cool adding at the same time 2 teaspoonsful of loaf sugar, ½ teaspoonful of pearlash and one teaspoonful of Common salt, stir until cold. The fluid must not be allowed to remain in a metallic vessel of any kind and must be kept in a cool place.

No. 2

Milk and water as in No. 1. Rub together with a little fresh cream into a soft batter. One tablespoonful each of good sweet rye flour, ground rice and pure starch which add to the milk and water as soon as they begin to boil. Boil for 5 mins. stirring constantly, remove from the fire and add 3 teaspoonsful of loaf sugar, ½ teaspoonful of pearlash, 1 teaspoonful of salt. Same precaution as No. 1.

No. 3

Milk and water as No. 1. When they begin to boil add one tablespoonful of flour, 2 of starch, 2 of carbonate of magnesia made into batter with milk. Boil gently for 5 minutes stirring constantly, pour into an earthen vessel to cool and add one teaspoonful of gum arabic dissolved in a little warm water, ½ teaspoonful of pearlash, one teaspoonful of salt and one tablespoonful of pure honey. Stir until cold, same precaution as No. 1. Dose of all three ½pt. a dose or 3pts. a day. Use No. 1 two weeks, No. 2 two weeks, No. 3 three weeks.

Rheumatism

23

First take a warm bath with salt in, then use pills made as follows: ½ scruple aloes, 3 grains opium, syrup of buckthorn, weight of one pill, 24 grains quinine, 1drm. iodide of potash, 2oz. distilled water. Dose: 1 pill at bedtime. For draught use 1drm. tincture of guaiacum, ½drm. tincture of aloes, 3 drops turpentine, 8 grains compound powder of ipecacuanha, 1½oz. camphor mixtur, 1oz. wine of colchicum seeds. Dose: 1 tablespoonful 3 time a day.

Warming Plaster
39

7oz. Burgundy pitch, melt and add 1oz. cantharides and a little camphor, for chest and head pains.

Icing for Cakes

1lb. sifted loaf sugar with whites of 3 eggs, beat well then add the juice of 6 lemons, keep beating until it becomes very light, if too stiff add a little more white of egg, if too soft more sugar, it is then ready for use.

Ground Rice Pudding

1qt. milk, 6oz. rice, stir this over the fire till thick, take it off put in piece of butter size of walnut, when just cold add 8 yolks of eggs, 4 whites well beaten, rasp the peel of lemon and put it to some sugar with the juice then mix all together, puff paste at the bottom of dish, bake ½ hour.

Plum Pudding

6oz. suet, 6oz. raisins, 3oz. sultanas, 6oz. currants, ½lb. apples, ¼lb. moist sugar, 3oz. bread, 3oz. flour, ½oz. blanched almonds grated, ½oz. spices, cloves, cinnamon, nutmeg and ginger, 3oz. mixed peel, ½pt. milk, 6 eggs. Beat up eggs and spices together, mix the milk by degrees then add ingredients working to smooth paste. Boil 12 hours.

Light Pudding

1qt. bread crumbs covered with water, then drain off at once, beat an egg with 2oz sugar, little salt and nutmeg, add 1pt. milk, ¼lb. raisins. Mix well. Bake 1 hour.

Marmalade Pudding

½lb. bread crumbs, 6 oz. beef suet, 3oz. sugar, 3oz. marmalade, the grated rind of lemon and juice, teaspoonful carb soda, mix then put in mold and steam for 3½ hours. Serve with sauce.

Tonic
40

Pour hot water on a handful of gentian chips when cold, strain and add one scruple of citrate of iron, 2 fluid drms elixir of vitrol, 6 fluid drms of tincture columbo, 5½oz. decolion bark, 3 fluid oz. of tincture of bark, 1 scruple aromatic confection, 1drm. aromatic spirit of ammonia, compound tincture of cinnamon and orange syrup each 2drms, infusion of cascarilla 5oz, sulphuric acid 2drms, syrup of ginger 6 drms, syrup of tolic ½drm. Dose: wine glass full 3 times a day.

Eye Plaster

1drm. conserve of roses, for inflamation.

Raspberry or Strawberry Cream

1½pt. fresh fruit beaten well with ½lb. loaf sugar and the juice of a lemon. Stir it to 1½pt. cream and milk, put cream first till it bears a fine froth.

Worm Mixture

25

1drm. populin, 20 grains santonin, 4oz. tinct pink root, 1pt. neutralising mixture. Rub the santonin in the mixture until throughly mixed and then add the other ingredients. Dose: from 30 to 40 drops every half hour until it acts on the bowels as a purge. If worms are not removed repeat dose for 2 to 3 days.

Asparagus and Eggs

Take cold boiled asparagus, cut the tender part up into pieces, place in buttered dish, season with pepper, salt and sugar, break fresh eggs over without breaking yolk, put a few lumps of butter and bake in quick oven till the eggs are cooked.

A Delicious Dish	6 baking pears, ½lb. sugar, ½pt. wine, 8 whole cloves, ½ lemon, ½oz. gelatine. Peel pears and cut in quarters, put in dish with sugar, cloves and water to cover if not covered with wine. Stew till tender then take the pears and put in dish for table to ½pt. of the liquor. Add the gelatine, juice and grated rind of lemon and wine, let these boil quickly for 5 mins. Strain over the pears and set in cool place.
Cheese Tartlets	Take 2oz. of finely grated cheese, beat it up in a bowl with the yolks of 2 eggs, take pepper, salt, cayenne and nutmeg to suit taste, very little of nutmeg and cayenne, then work in 3 tablespoonsful of cream, line pastry pans with puff paste and fill with the mixture. Bake in moderate oven.
To Perfume Linen	Rose leaves dried, powder of cloves, mace scraped. Put in bag.
Golden Balls	1oz. sweet almonds, 2oz. bitter almonds blanched and pounded, 3 tablespoonsful of jam, 2oz. fine bread crumbs, 2 well whisked eggs. Mix well together then add 1oz. butter melted to the consistency of cream, half fill some buttered cups with the mixture and bake 20 mins. in gentle oven.
Honey Soap	Cut 2 tabs yellow soap into shreds, put in saucepan on fire with just as much water as will keep it from burning. When quite melted add ¼lb. honey stirring till it boils then take off and add 3 pennyworth[41], of oil of Cinnamon, pour into dish and cut into squares when cold.
Chapped Hands	1½oz. spermaceti[42], 1½oz. white wax, scrape into earthern jam pot, add 6drms. of pounded camphor and pour on the whole 4 tablespoonsful of olive oil. Let it stand before fire till melted. Use before going to bed, cover pot lightly over.
Indigestion Gingerbread	3lbs. ervalenta[43], 3lbs. best rye meal, 2lbs. treacle, 1lb. moist sugar, 1oz. powdered ginger, one teaspoonful carb soda, a few caraway seeds. The ervalenta and rye to be well mixed and sieved, sugar and soda mixed same then mix the whole together, add as much warm water to the treacle as will make up the meal, work in usual way and bake in quick oven. The lentils are the ervum lens not the common lentil.
Orange Bitters	Take the rind of 18 oranges, add 1½lbs. sugar candy and 1 gall. gin, let it stand 2 months, then bottle for use.
Warts	The burnt ashes of the bark of the common willow mixed with strong vinegar and applied to the parts will remove all warts, corns etc.

Warts and Corns
Apply the leaves of the great celandine or letterwort[30]. Apply till removed.

Preserve Rabbit Skins
Pulverise well and mix a spoonfull of alum[11] and 2 of salt-petre[44]. After sprinkling the powder on the flesh side of the skin, lay the two flesh sides together, fold up and hang in a dry place. In three days take it down and scrape well with a blunt knife till clean. When they become stiff draw each skin through a small ring until it is soft.

Heartburn	5oz. water, 2drms. carbonate of ammonia, 1oz. syrup of orange peel. Mix well.
Dry Yeast	In a pint of water boil a handful of hops till 1 third of the water is boiled away, pour this boiling hot through a sieve onto two tablespoonsful of sifted flour. Stir the mixture till smooth then add a cup of fresh yeast. When it has risen pour it into a bowl and mix it with corn meal till it is a firm dough, cut into shapes and dry in the shade. When thoroughly dry put them in a paper bag and hang in dry place. For use dissolve 1 cake in a cup of water, stir in flour to form a batter and when light set sponge.
Hoarseness	A piece of flanel dipped in brandy and applied to the chest and covered with a dry flanel is to be worn at night.
Whooping Cough	Equal quantities of castor oil and molasses well mixed together. Dose: 1 teaspoonful when cough is troublesome. Good for croup.
To Test Water	Fill a clean white cup with the water and add 10 drops of pure dilute sulphuric acid. Stir with glass rod and add weak solution of permanganate of potassium and let it stand some time. If pure colour will remain, if not will turn colourless.
Corns [45]	First pare it then apply a little lint saturated with turps every night at bedtime, keeping on all night. Will cure in 4 days.
Chilblains	Take common red pepper or cayenne and put into spirits[46] sufficient to make quite strong and bathe the affected parts freely.
Tincture of Roses	Take the leaves of the common rose, place them without pressing into a large mouthed bottle, pour some good spirits of wine over them. Seal the bottle securely and let them remain in a dry place for a month or two.
Fig Pudding	8oz. bread crumbs, 6oz. beef suet, 1 teaspoonful of warm milk, 2 eggs well beaten, 4oz. figs finely minced, 4oz. lump sugar. Place the figs in the milk by the fire then mix all and boil 4 hours. Serve with sweet sauce.
Waterproof Boots	Rub well with castor oil, about a tablespoonful to each boot, varnish soles and heels with oak varnish.
Ox Tongue	Take a fresh ox-tongue, stick with cloves and roast. Serve with port wine sauce and currant jelly. It makes an excellent dish.

To Improve the Voice

2drms. beeswax, 3drms. balsam of copaiba$_{31}$, 4drms. powdered liquorice root. Melt the copaiba with the wax in an earthern pipkin. When melted remove from the fire and while in a liquid state mix the powdered liquorice. Make pills 3 grains each and take 3 or 4 a day.

To Remove Moles

47

4oz. each of dried tops of rosemary, sage leaves and flowers of lavender, ½oz. cloves, 3drms. camphor, 6pts. distilled water, macerate with heat for 14 days then filter. Apply a drop twice a day to the moles until removed.

Chalk Ointment

Mix as much chalk as possible into lard so as to form a thick ointment. Use for burns etc.

Dry Soap

14ozs. ground soda, ¼oz. ground borax, 2 ozs. soda ash. Mix well.

Alum Water

Keep a cup of alum water close at hand for cut fingers and bruises of all kinds wrapped in cloth wet in the alum water. Will heal with a rapidity truly wonderful.

Hair Wash

4drms. vinegar of cantharides[49], 4drms. glycerine, 2drms. tincture of quinine, 4oz. orange water, 4oz. rose water. To be applied to the roots of the hair night and morning.

Indigestion

1oz. cascarilla bark to be well bruised, 4drms. carb soda, pour on 1pt. of boiling water. When cool strain and bottle. Dose: 2 tablespoonsful 3 times a day. [50]

Ginger Wine

1 gall. water, 2oz. ginger bruised, 3lbs. sugar, ½lb. raisins, 2 lemons. Bruise ginger and put in barrel, cut raisins and add cut lemons well squeezed, add all to above then add sugar and water, ½oz. german yeast[51]. Keep in warm place and stir daily for one week. Put away in cool place, air tight ready for bottling in 6 weeks.

Eye Lotion

Chamomile flowers ½oz., boiling water ½pt. Infuse for ½ hour then strain and use. This is a mild eye wash.

Decayed Teeth

[52]

Dissolve in a well stopped bottle ¼oz. gum mastic in a quantity of sulphuric ether barely sufficient for the purpose. Saturate with this solution a small piece of cotton the size of the cavity. Gently press the cotton into it. This is a very good remedy.

Deafness

5 drops sassafras oil[53], ½oz. sweet oil, mix and drop into the ear once or twice a day.

Piles

[54]

¼oz. cream of tartar, ¼oz. milk of sulphur, in a small quantity of treacle as possible. Dose: one teaspoonful.

Blood Spilling

[55]

Is stopped immediately by drinking sage tea sweetened with honey.

Blood to Renew

[55]

Boil watercress for 10 minutes and drink the water in milk.

Bleeding of the Nose

[55]

Nettle juice steeped in a little lint and put up the nostrils will stay bleeding of the nose when all other remedies fail.

Cuts

A bruised geranium leaf applied to a cut quickly heals it, or powdered rice sprinkled on a cut or wound stops bleeding at once, or for a cut that festers apply turpentine.

Diptheria Is cured by drinking the best olive oil freely.

[56]

Dropsy  If it can be cured at all it is cured by foxglove[57] and broom in small quantities, used as tea a wineglassful 3 times a day is invaluable.

Liver Complaint Boil gently ¼ tub of stone brimstone in 1qt. of water. Bottle when cold. Dose: one wineglassful twice a day.

Ringworm Citrine ointment is a quick cure for ringworm or common soda, dissolved in hot water and applied to the ringworm, or lime water from gasworks used in the same manner.

Spasms For windy spasms drink hot ginger tea with a pinch of cayenne or carb soda in it.

Bowel Complaint Black currant tea is invaluable.

Boils and Carbuncles Get the leaves of the round leafed pyrold[35] or pear leafed wintergreen and of the decoction, make a poultice and apply to parts affected.

Worms	20 drops turpentine in a tablespoonful of water before breakfast for several days, children should be given 4 to 6 drops in a little milk with 2 or 3 drops of essence of peppermint.
Teething	On children cutting teeth nothing answers so well as rubbing their gums several times with syrup of poppies.
Offensive Breath	½ teaspoonful of powdered charcoal in a wineglass of water 3 times a day and a free use of fruits is invaluable.
Blood to Cleanse	A very important drink is made as follows: 1oz. horehound$_3$, 1oz. burdock, 1oz. hops, 1oz. gentian, 5oz. Ginger, 2oz. spanish juice to 5 galls. water. Boil 1 hour, strain and ferment 24 hours then bottle. For every impurity of the blood or to keep a person in health, no better drink can be had.
Bunions	Paint them night and morning with tincture of iodine.
Eczema	This is one of the most difficult skin diseases to cure, but by applying and persevering with vaseline ointment it will be found to have a wonderful effect over this most obstinate disease.
Hair Falling Off	Use vaseline ointment, it is a good restorative.

5 8

Sea Sickness	Before going on board take a substantial meal and on voyage one teaspoonful of the fluid extract of cocoa in a little water every one or two hours.
Neuralgia	The simplest and best remedy is to wear well pounded brimstone on the sole of the foot contrary to the pain side or cayenne sprinkled on hot flannel afford instant relief to persons troubled with neuralgia or apply very hot hops in bag.
Small Pox	1oz. cream tartar, 1pt. boiling water, drink at intervals when cold.
Ground Rice Cake	½lb. ground rice, ½lb. sugar, ½lb. butter, beaten to a cream. ¼lb. flour, 20 drops essence of lemon, ½ teaspoonful carb soda. Mix dry ingredients first then add butter and 4 eggs. Bake in moderate oven, line with note paper.

**To Cure
Baldness**

1oz. lac sulphur, ½oz. sugar of lead, 5 grains sulphate of copper, ½pt. pure water. Mix and filter. Add 7oz. rose water, 1oz. each of bergamot, cinnamon, jessamine and peppermint. Bath the head in this twice a day and give a cold shower bath once or twice a week.

For Cold and Cough 5 9	½oz. elixir of vitriol, ½oz. white ether, ½ lb. lump sugar, ½pt. hot water. Dissolve sugar first and let it cool then add to vitriol and ether. Dose: eggcupful; if too strong for use add more cold water. A sure cure.
Arrow Root Jelly	Stir a tablespoonful of arrow root into a cupful of cold water, pour in 1pt. of boiling water, let it stand 7 mins. and then sweeten and flavour to suit the taste.
Potato Yeast	2 potatoes grated, ½pt. boiling water, 2oz. sugar, teaspoonful salt. When cool add ½ cupful good yeast, let it rise. When light bottle and cork.
Currant Bread	1 stone flour, 2lbs. sugar, 5lbs. currants, 1½ozs. lard, 2ozs. salt, 2ozs. barm.
Mince Meat 6 0	2½lbs. suet, 2½lbs. apples, 2lbs. raisins, 2lbs. currants, ½ minced peel, 2lbs. moist sugar, 2lbs. nutmegs, 3 lemons, grated and juice. Put in cool place till wanted.
Seed or Currant Bread 6 0	1 stone flour, 3½lbs. lard, 3½lbs. currants, 3½lbs. sugar, ¾ peel, 2oz. salt, 4oz. barm, 2oz. seeds, 2 eggs. Mix well with new milk, omit seeds or currants as required.
Currant Bread	1 stone flour, 5lbs. currants, 2½lbs. lard, ½oz. peel, 6oz. barm, ½oz. seeds, little nutmeg, 2 eggs. Mix with milk.
Pound Cake	1lb. butter beaten to a cream, 1lb. sifted loaf sugar, 1lb. flour, 8 egg yolks and whites beaten separately, ¼oz. caraway seeds, line tin, bake in moderate oven.
Test for Plate 6 1	Clean the surface, place 1 drop of cold solution of bi-chromatic of potash in nitric acid, wash off at once with cold water. If silver a blood red spot, if germain silver or metal the stain is brown or black.
Plain Cake	¾lb. flour, ¼lb. sugar, ¼lb. currants, 2 teaspoonsful baking powder, 1 egg, ½pt. milk. Powder and milk to be mixed when going into oven.
Good Cake	1½lbs. bread dough, ½lb. currants, ½oz. seeds, 6oz. sugar, 3 eggs, ½lb. butter, mix as bun paste.
To Sweeten Rank Butter	To 3lbs. butter, 2½drms. carb soda, for making butter the soda is to be added after all the milk is washed out and it is ready for making up.

Seed Bread   1lb. flour, 3oz. lard, ½lb. sugar, 1½oz. baking powder, ½oz. seeds, 2 eggs, ½pt. milk, salt, 1oz. cut peel.

French Cake   Out of 2lbs. flour take ½lb., make hole in centre and put ¼oz. yeast mixed with a little warm water, make it into a sponge and place it well wrapped up in a warm place. When risen make a hole in rest of flour and add 1lb. butter, 6 eggs. Work to soft sponge, cut up ¼lb. each of raisins and currants and ¼lb. sugar, mix well and prove bake in moderate oven for 1¼ hours.

Cheese Sandwiches   2 thirds cheese, 1 butter, add a little cream, pound all together then spread on slices of brown bread and cut in squares.

California Cakes 6 2	1pt. flour, 1pt. ind meal, 1pt. milk, 2 eggs, 1 teaspoonful carbonate of soda, 2 teaspoonsful cream of tartar, 4 tablespoonsful of sugar, small piece of butter, mix eggs and milk together, add sugar and butter well beaten, then flour and meal a little at a time, mix cream of tartar in flour, and soda in milk. Bake in pans and serve hot.
Cake	2lbs. flour, ½lb. sugar, ½lb. butter, 1oz. carb soda, ½oz. tart acid, 1pt. milk.
Toothache	Place a little horseradish, scraped on the tooth and round the gum, sure relief.
Cake	2lbs. flour, ¼lb. butter, ½lb. sugar, ½lb. currants, 6 large teaspoonsful of baking powder. Rub in and mix with 2 eggs and milk.
Shrewsbury Cakes	1lb. flour, ½lb. sugar, ½lb. butter, 2 eggs, mix into a paste with a glass of white wine, roll it out thick and cut with wine glass.
Camphorated Oil	Dissolve ½oz. camphor in 2oz. olive oil.
Baking Powder 6 3	1½oz. carb soda, ½oz. tart acid, 1½oz. alum, ¼oz. cream of tartar, 3oz. volatile ammonia, 5 tubs - 10oz. flour rice, to sell at 6d. per pound.
Baking Powder No. 2 6 3	1oz. tart acid, 1oz. carb soda, 1oz. alum, 2½ oz. rice flour, to sell at 10d. per pound.
Baking Powder No. 3 6 3	½oz. cream tartar, 1½oz. carb soda, 1oz. tart acid, ½ oz. alum, ½oz. ground rice, 3½oz. rice flour. Costs 6d. to sell at 10d.
Fruit Salt 6 4	2oz. sherbert powder, 2oz. epsom salts, 2oz. carb soda, 1½oz. tart acid, 1oz. cream tartar, 3oz. sugar crushed lump.
Snowdon Pudding	½lb. flour, ½lb. bread crumbs, ¼lb. suet, a pinch of salt, 2 tablespoonsful of sugar, 2 of marmalade, 1 teaspoonful baking powder, 1 egg, little milk. Grease the mould and dredge it with bread crumbs, boil 2 hours.
Table Beer 6 5	5 galls. water, 1oz. linseed, 2oz. gentian, 2oz. spanish juice, 2oz. carrander seeds, 2 tubs sugar, 2oz. liquorice root.

To Shrink Wool All wool before knitting should be thrown in cold water. A little alum in the water will set the colour if inclined to come off.

Sherbert Powder 6 4	2oz. loaf sugar, ¼oz. tart acid, ¼oz. cream of tartar, ½oz. carb soda.
Fruit Salt No. 2 6 4 6 3	4oz. epsom salts, 3oz. tart acid, 3oz. carb soda, 3oz. cream tartar, ¼oz. magnesia, ½oz. sugar. To sell at 1½d. per oz.
Currant Bread	1½ stone flour, 4½lbs. currants, ½oz. seeds, 3lbs. sugar, 2¾lbs. lard, 6oz. peel, 1qt. milk, ½oz. barm.
To Restore Black Cloth 6 6	Bruised galls 1oz., logwood 2oz., green vitriol ½oz., water 5qts. Boil for 2 hours and strain.
Lime and Oil 6 7	Equal parts of linseed oil and lime water. Shake well. Apply to burns, scolds etc.
Egg and Custard Powder	2oz. ground rice flour, ¼oz. tart acid, 6oz. carb soda, 1oz. lentil flour. Crush and mix well.
Lemon Kali	2oz. ground lump sugar, ¼oz. tart acid, 6oz. carb soda, well crush and mix, then add 20 drops of essence of lemon.
Raspberry Kali	Add 20 drops of essence of raspberry.
Orange Kali	Add 20 drops of oil of orange.
Ginger Kali	Add 20 drops of essence of ginger.
Citron Kali	Add 20 drops of oil of citron[6].
Lime Juice Kali	Add 15 drops of oil of limes.
Baking Powder No. 4. 6 3	1lb. rice flour, ½oz. carb soda, ¼oz. tart acid. To sell at 10d. per pound.
Cocoa Nut Biscuits	Grate 2oz. cocoa nut mix with ¼lbs. powdered white sugar, and the whites of 3 eggs previously beaten to a froth, drop small pieces of this mixture on paper, place in a baking tin in a slow oven for about 10 mins.

Stomach Plaster for Cough

1oz. each of bees wax, burgundy pitch[39] and resin. Melt together in a pipkin and stir in ¾oz. turps, ½oz. mace spread on sheeps leather, grate nutmeg over it and apply warm.

Prince Albert Pudding

6oz. flour, 6oz. butter, beaten to a cream, 4 eggs, 6oz. raisins, chopped fine, 6oz. pounded loaf sugar, flavour with either lemon or almond. Boil 3 hours.

Chilblains

68

Rub the affected parts night and morning with a lotion made of 1oz. opodeloc, ¼oz. cajuput oil, ¼oz. tincture of cantharides. Editors note: opodeloc is a soap liniment.

Ringworm Ointment

69

Sulphate of zinc 1drm, simple cerate 1oz., after washing the head.

Tooth Powder

70

3oz. prepared chalk, 1oz. powdered borax, 1oz. powdered orris root, 1drm. powdered cardemon seeds, 1oz. white sugar, well mixed to be used with a tooth brush night and morning, flavour as desired.

Liquid Blacking

4oz. ivory black, 3oz. coarse sugar, tablespoonful of sweet oil, 1pt. vinegar. Mix gradually.

Liquid Blacking No. 2

71

2oz. Ivory black in fine powder, 1½oz. treacle, ¼pt. sperm oil. Rub the black and oil well together, add the treacle and mix.

Black Reviver

72

1qt. vinegar infuse, 1oz. iron filings, 10oz. copperas, 1oz. ground logwood, 3oz. bruised galls, mix well and strain.

Rock Cakes

Rub ¼lb. butter into 1lb. of flour, mix in ¼lb. of castor sugar, ½lb. currants, 1oz. peel finely chopped, the grated peel of ½ a lemon, 1 tablespoonful of baking powder, add 2 eggs. In order that the cakes may have a rocky shape the paste must be very stiff, if too moist the cakes will be flat, if the eggs are not sufficient to work up the paste add a few drops of milk. Flour a baking sheet, with your finger put little pieces of the cake at equal distances taking care to drop them lightly so that they retain a proper shape.

Feather Cake

Beat to a cream ½ cup full of butter, 2 cups full of sugar, 1 of milk with a teaspoonful of cream and one of soda dissolved in it, beat well together then add 1 cup of flour with a teaspoonful of cream of tartar rubbed in it, and the well beaten yolk of 3 eggs. Beat the whites separately till stiff, add them and two more cups of flour to the other ingredients, beat well. Butter two tins, pour in the cakes and bake 20 mins.

Mince Meat

73

3lbs. apples, 2lbs. raisins, 2lbs. currants, ¾ candid peel, ¾ suet, 2 tubs sugar.

35

Burning Feet   Discard light and tight boots then take 1 pt. bran, 1oz.
bicarbonate of soda add 1 gall. hot water. When cool enough
soak the feet for 15 mins. Repeat every night for a week.
Make fresh after weeks use.

Currant   1 stone flour, 4lbs. currants, 2oz. lard, ½oz. peel, ½oz.
Bread   seeds, 5oz. barm, 4 eggs, 1pt. milk, 2½lbs. sugar, 3oz.
baking powder.

Lemon Cheese 7 4	1lb. butter, 1lb. sugar, 2 lemons (juice), 4 eggs, the 4 yolks but only 2 whites.
Lemon Curd 7 4	¼lb. butter, 4 eggs, 1lb. loaf sugar, 3 lemons.
Ginger Beer Powder	Fine sugar 2drms., ground ginger 6 grains, carb soda 26 grains, tart acid 28 grains, dissolve all in ½ tumbler of water.
Dandelion Coffee	Coffee 3 parts, dandelion 1 part, chicory 1 part. Grind and mix.
Seed Bread 7 5	1 stone flour, 2¾lbs. lard, 3½lbs. sugar, ¾ peel, 5oz. barm, 2oz. seeds, 2 eggs, 3oz. baking powder, milk.

Rheumatics 4 8	1lb. treacle, 1oz. flour, 1oz. cream tartar, ¼lb. turkey rhubarb powdered, ¼lb. ginger powdered, 1drm. gum guaiacum powdered. Dose 2 tablespoonsful going to bed. A nobleman gave £500 for this recipe.

Meat	How to distinguish good from bad meat. It should be firm and elastic when touched, scarcely moistening the finger. It should have a marbled appearance from the ramifications of little layers of fat among the muscles, and no odour beyond that which characterises fresh meat. When allowed to stand for some time the surface becomes dry. Bad meat on the other hand is wet and sodden and continues so, it has moreover a sickly odour. When the flesh has a deep purple tint it is probable that the animal has not been slaughtered[76], or else that it has suffered from some fever.
Ointment Healing	1oz. mutton suet, 1oz. resin, ½oz. olive oil. Put in earthen jar and dissolve by heat.
Butter	When butter has been mixed with tallow it may be usually detected by melting a little of the butter in a spoon and smelling it, when the smell of the tallow may be at once perceived.
Flexible Glue	Dissolve 1 tub of good glue in water after the usual manner, take 4oz. arrowroot and mix with cold water to the consistence of cream, stir this into boiling glue and mix well, then stir in 2½oz. glycerine, mix throughly, add ½oz. carbolic acid and colour with anniline to any desired shade. Apply lukewarm with flat brush.
Bacilicon Ointment [77]	Yellow wax and yellow rosin, 10oz. pitch, 5oz. malt and add 10oz. linseed oil when taken from the fire.
Cough Mixture [78]	4oz. blood root, 1oz. wine of antimony, 2oz. syrup of tolu, 1oz. syrup of squill, 4drms. wine of ipecac, 6drms. paregoric, 3oz. gum mucilage arabic, 5oz. molasses, 1oz. tincture lobelia, 1drm. oil of spearmint, 4oz. castor oil. Dose: 1 teaspoonful 3 times a day, if very bad every four hours.
Currant Bread	The following are very good for public teas. 1 stone flour, 4lbs. currants, 2¼lbs. lard, ½ peel, ½oz. seeds, 6oz. barm, 2 eggs, 2½ tubs sugar, mix with milk, 2oz. salt.
Seed Bread	1 stone flour, 3lbs. lard, 3½lbs. sugar, ¾ peel, 2oz. salt, 6oz barm, 2oz. seeds, 2 eggs, mix with milk.
Ointment Bittersweet [79]	2oz. bark of bittersweet, cover with spirits of wine and add 8oz. unsalted butter, simmer and strain. Excellent for swelled breasts, tumors, ulcers, etc. Apply twice a day.

Enlarged Liver Enlargement of the liver is a dangerous complaint. If it is severe the diet should be of the simplest, drink nothing very hot and make free use of stewed prunes for a fortnight.

Rich Pound Cake

10oz. fine flour, ½lb. butter, the grated end of one lemon, 2oz. chopped peel, 3oz. currants, 3oz. sultanas, put the butter into a large bowl, beat it with the hand to a cream then put in the sugar and go on pounding, then add a quarter of the flour, one egg and so on till the eggs and flour are all in, work well with the hand, grate in the lemon, add the peel and fruit and mix all well together. Oil the cake tin well and tie a band of oiled paper outside it. Bake in a moderate oven for two hours.

Ointment Yellow

80

8oz. yellow wax, 3oz. burgundy pitch, 4oz. venice turps, 1oz. linseed oil, 8oz. resin. First melt resin to which add the wax and the pitch, when whole is melted, remove from the fire and slowly put in oil stirring well till cold. This is good for healing cuts, absesses and local affections.

Black Salve

81

1pt. olive oil, ½oz. resin, ½oz. bees wax, ¼oz. venice turpentine, melt then gradually add 2oz. red lead while on the fire. Boil slowly till a dark brown when remove and add 1drm. powdered camphor when it is nearly cold. This is a superior healing salve for burns, scalds etc. Spread on linen and renew daily.

Ointment Green

82

3oz. each yellow wax and rosin, 6oz. venice turps, 1oz. powdered verdigris, 6oz. lard. Melt first the rosin etc. as before. These ointments are very efficacious in healing cuts, absesses and local affections of any kind.

Family Salve

83

1lb. lard, 3oz. white lead, 3oz. red lead, 3oz. bees wax, 2oz. black rosin, 4oz. turps. All but turps to be put in a pan and boiled ¾ hour. The turps to be put in just before it is done and give it a gentle boil afterwards. This is an excellent cure for burns, sores or ulcers, as it first drains, then heals. Excellent for all wounds.

Ointment Spermaceti

84

1pt. olive oil, 3oz. each white wax and spermaceti. Melt them with a gentle heat and briskly stir together till cold. If 2drms. of camphor previously rubbed with a small quantity of oil be added to the above it will make the white camphorated ointment.

Ointment Sulphur

85

4oz. lard, 1½oz. flour of sulphur, 2drms. crude salammoniac, 12 drops essence of lemon. Mix into ointment, the best for itch.

Hair   Rum applied to the hair keeps it exceedingly clean and promotes growth more than oil or anything known.

For Cold and Cough $\frac{1}{2}$oz. elixar of vitrol$_{40}$, $\frac{1}{2}$oz. white ether$_{86}$, $\frac{1}{2}$lb. lump sugar, $\frac{1}{2}$pt. hot water, dissolve sugar first and let it cool then add to vitrol and ether. Dose: eggcupful, if too strong for use add more cold water. A sure cure.

Currant Bread	1 stone flour, 5lbs. currants, 2½lbs. lard, ½ peel, 6oz. barm, ½oz. seeds, little nutmeg, 2 eggs. Mix with milk.
Pound Cake	1lb. butter beaten to a cream, 1lb. sifted loaf sugar, 1lb. flour, 8 eggs yolks and whites beaten separately, ¼oz. caraway seeds, line tin, bake in moderate oven.
Plain Cake	¾lb. flour, ¼lb. sugar, ¼lb. currants, 2 teaspoonfuls baking powder, 1 egg, ½pt. milk, powder and milk to be mixed when going into oven.
Good Cake	1½lbs. bread dough, ½lb. currants, ½oz. seeds, 6oz. sugar, 3 eggs, ½lb. butter, mix as bun paste.
French Cake	Out of 2lbs. flour take ½lb. make hole in centre and put in ¼oz. yeast mixed with a little warm water make it into a sponge and place it well wrapped up in a warm place, when risen make a hole in rest of flour and add 1lb. butter, 6 eggs, work to soft sponge, cut up ¼lb. each of raisins and currants and ¼lb. sugar, mix well and prove bake in moderate oven 1¼ hours.
Cheese Sandwiches	2 thirds cheese, 1 butter, add a little cream, pound all together then spread on slices of brown bread and cut in squares.
Hare Soup	The bones and remains of roast hare, gravy and forcemeat, 1lb. gravy beef, 2oz. bacon, 2 onions, 4 cloves, 1 bouquet of herbs, 12 peppercorns, 3 quarts of water, 1 glass of claret or port, a teaspoonful of red currant jelly, 2oz. of bread crumbs. Cut the meat from the hare, and the bones into small joints. Cut up the gravy beef. The bacon should be cut into small dice. Make the bacon very hot in a saucepan, put in the meat and joints of hare, and fry them brown. If not enough fat to fry in, add a little dripping or butter. Take up the joints of hare and meat, make the fat very hot once again, and fry the onions sliced and the herbs. When a golden brown, return the meat and bones, add the water, and bring to the boil. Add a little salt, and simmer gently for four hours. Skim well, and, if possible, allow to go cold, and then remove all traces of grease. Take the meat from the hare, pass through a mincing machine, and rub as much as possible through a sieve; add this to the hare soup. Return to the saucepan, make very hot. Soak the bread in water, squeeze all water from it in a cloth, and put into the soup. If not sufficiently thick, blend a tablespoon of cornflour with cold water and strain in. Stir with a whisk to keep it smooth, and boil up. Add the wine and red currant jelly, and serve at once. If there is forcemeat left from the roast hare, cut it into nice-sized dice, and add to the soup just before serving.

Breasts
When hard poultice with roasted mashed turnips mixed with a little oil of roses. Change at least twice a day, taking care to keep the breasts warm with flannels. For sore and swollen breasts, boil a handful of camomile and mallows in a pint of milk and water and foment with it as hot as possible between two flannels.

Arrow Root Jelly
Stir a tablespoonful of arrow root$_{87}$ into a cupful of cold water, pour in 1pt. of boiling water let it stand 7 mins. and then sweeten and flavour to suit the taste.

Potato Yeast
2 potatoes grated, ½pt. boiling water, 2oz. sugar, teaspoonful salt, when cool add ½ cupful good yeast let it rise, when light bottle and cork.

Currant Bread
1 stone flour, 2lbs. sugar, 5lbs. currants, 1½lbs. lard, 2oz. salt, 2oz. barm.

Seed or Currant Bread
1 stone flour, 3½lbs. lard, 3½lbs. currants, 3½lbs. sugar, ¾ peel, 2oz. salt, 4oz. barm, 2oz. seeds, 2 eggs. Mix well with new milk, omit seeds or currants as required.

Hunters' Soup

The bones of cooked game, 1 slice of ham or bacon cooked or uncooked, 1oz. of butter or dripping, 1 dessertspoonful of currypowder, 2 medium onions, 2 tomatoes (optional), 1 quart of water or second stock. Take the bones or remains of cold cooked game, cut scraps of meat off and chop the bones and carcase across. Put them on a dish and shake the currypowder and a dessertspoonful of flour over them. Chop the onions, make the dripping very hot in a saucepan and fry the onions a light brown. Then put in the game bones, flour, and currypowder, also the ham cut up small. Stir well over the fire for three or four minutes, taking care it does not burn. Now put in the tomatoes sliced, and the water or stock. Bring to boiling point, stirring to prevent the flour going into lumps. Simmer very gently by the side of the fire for two hours. Skim well and strain the soup into a basin. Again remove any trace of fat, return to the saucepan, make very hot, season as required with pepper, salt, and if liked a little port wine, and half a teaspoonful of red currant jelly. Serve.

Partridge Pudding

2 partridges, 2 hard-boiled eggs, some button mushrooms (optional), a good suet crust, and some small forcemeat balls. For the suet crust take ½lb. of flour, 4oz. of suet finely chopped, 1 teaspoonful baking powder, ½ teaspoonful of salt. Chop the suet with the flour, add the other ingredients, and mix to a very dry dough with cold water. Roll out, and line a buttered pudding basin, keeping some pastry for the lid. For the inside mixture: Cut the partridges into nice joints and lightly brown in a little butter. Put into the lined basin with the eggs, cut in quarters, and dust in a teaspoonful of flour seasoned with pepper and salt. The mushrooms and forcemeat balls (if being used) should be distributed between the layers of game. Pour in a cup of gravy water, moisten the edge of the pastry with water, and lay on the lid. Tie a cloth over the top in the usual way, and boil for 2½ hours. Serve with a dinner napkin.

A Christmas Game Pie

1 pheasant, or 3 partridges, 1lb. of sausages, 1lb. of veal or beef, 3 hard boiled eggs, ¼lb. of lean ham. Puff pastry or flaky to cover the pie. These pies were more generally made in a rather large and not too deep pie dish. The small piece of ham should be put into warm water and boiled gently for ten minutes. This parboils it and prevents it discolouring the other meats by turning them red. The game must be cut into nice sized joints and the bones removed. This is easily done with a sharp knife scraping close to the bone from the inside; each joint should be seasoned with a little pepper, salt and cayenne and folded into a neat shape. The sausages are best brought to the boil, then plunged into cold water for a few seconds to set them. The skin should then be slit with a sharp

44

knife and removed. The bones of the game must be put into 1½ pints of water, with an onion, a blade of mace, a small bunch of herbs and a few allspice and peppercorns, and stewed for a couple of hours to make stock. Now line the edges of the dish well down with pastry. Lay in some slices of the sausages at the bottom then some pieces of veal and strips of ham then some joints of game. Season each layer and repeat until the pie is well built up. It should have a small cup in the centre. Add a cupful of the stock and cover with the puff pastry, decorating with large leaves making holes in the top which should be partly hidden by a pastry ornament. Brush over with egg. Bake in a quick oven for a few minutes to prevent the pastry from slipping, and as soon as it shows any sign of colouring cover with paper and bake on a moderate shelf for 2½ hours. Strain the stock and take ¾ pint, add 1 glass sherry to it (optional) and five sheets of leaf gelatine. Season to taste and strain in through the hole in the top. Serve when cold and the stock will be set in a jelly.

NOTES

1   ratafias — biscuit flavoured with almonds

2   volatile ammonia — a distillate of lemon oil, nutmeg oil and alcohol, with ammonia.

3   horehound — marrubium vulgare

4   tart — tartaric, tartaric acid or cream of tartar

5   carb soda — bicarbonate of soda

6   citron — obtained by the expression of lemon peel, a lemon flavouring

7   beware — chloroform and ether are anaesthetics

8   proud flesh — swellings, boils, etc.

9   the unit is not given but is assumed to be ¾lb. The use of glaziers' putty is to take benefit from the linseed oil, and the malleability of the putty is used as a casing for the hands

10   carbolic acid (phenol) is caustic to the skin

11   Alum — potassium aluminium sulphate — a powerful astringent

12   the extract of cabbage reads 'extract of skunk cabbage', which is a complete mystery to us.
blood root — Sanguinaria canadensis
pleurisy root — Asclepias tuberosa

13   Ladies slipper — Cypripedium ealoaolus
catnip — cat mint, Nepeta glechoma
scullcap — skullcap — Scuttellania galericulata, blue flower of meadows and riversides for 'nerves'

14   aloes — a purgative, having many varieties, a favourite herb since 1596
gamboge — a gum resin from Cambodia, a yellow pigment
colocynth — bitter apple, a purgative, possibly a reference to Colocasia, (Taro Root)

15   colcheum — meadow saffron, used for gout

16   tasmin — not known
belladonna — deadly nightshade, Atropa belladonna, contains an alkoloid atropine
conicum — Conium maculatum, hemlock, used by the Greeks as a capital punishment
senna — cassia, a popular purgative
fennel — a common herb used in culinary dishes, contains ethereal oil
marshmallow — Marsh marigold, Althaea officinus
Altogether a lethal mixture

17   It is not known what is meant by 'spirits', but it could be as simple as a salt water solution or is likely to be alcohol

18 scullcap — as 13 above
chamomile — Matricaria chamomilla, has ethereal oils, an old 'tea' favourite
boneset — comfrey — Symphytum officinale, also knitboro and bruisewort, being self explanatory
salerian — valerian?

19 gentian root — Gentiana lutea, contains alkiloids and tannias (used for flavouring Schnaps)
cardimon — cardamon, a spice from East India

20 under no circumstances should sulphuric acid be handled, and certainly not applied to the body in any form

21 sulphuric ether — sulphuric acid, see 20

22 pearlash — potassium carbonate

23 buckthorn — Rhammus cathartica, a strong purgative
iodie of potash — Potassium iodide
guaiacum — gum from shrubs native to the West Indies
ipecacuanha — root of a South American shrub, a purgative
aloes — see 14

24 Acitate of morphine — morphine acetate, a narcotic analgesic
cardamon — see 19

25 populin — not known
santonin — extract of santonica (wormwood), an anthelmintic (anti intestinal worms agent)
pink root — dianthus
neutralizing mixture —

26 guaiacum — see 23
galbanum — a gum resin
ipecacuanha — see 23

27 the quantities are assumed to be tubs, the original is not clear
cayberry — possibly the berry of the capsicum, cayenne
calmony — not known

28 tolu — balsam from a south American tree
squills — Urginea maritima, a sea onion used as an expectorant
paregoric — an 'elixir', of tincture of opium, flavoured and camphorated (narcotic)
ipecacuanha — see 23

29 acetate of morphine — see 24
antimonial wine — tartar emetic (potassium antimonial tartrate) in wine
blood root — see 12
ipecacuanha — see 23

30 letterwort — not known

31 copaiba — aromatic balsam

32 sublimed sulphur — sublimated sulphur
    sub-carbonate of potash — potassium carbonate
33 scammony — a convolvulus type of plant, violently purgative
    gamboge — as 14
    malefern is dried dryopteris filix-mas
34 extract of colombo — a bitter obtained from the root of jateorhiza
    palmata
35 pyrold — not known
36 cranesbill — Geranium, possibly sylvaticum, the Wood Crane's Bill,
    which contains tannin
    cohosh — dried root of Cimifuga racemosa, mild expectorant
    golden seal — dried roots of hydrastis canadensis
37 not the carcanoma as we understand it, but a skin condition
    poke weed — phytolaccas americana
    The French Brandy is an exotic antiseptic
38 A fortune for you if it works, but they never do!
    lac sulphur — milk of sulphur — precipitated sulphur
    sugar of lead — lead acetate, restricted for use in cosmetics
    sulphate of copper — blue vitriol, an emetic and wet dressing for
    exzema, etc.
    bergamot — extract from a type of citrous tree, used in Earl Grey's tea.
39 burgundy pitch — purified resinous exudate from Norway spruce
    (Christmas tree)
    camtharides — same as 49
40 gentian chips — chopped gentian root, compound tincture of cinchora
    citrate of iron — probably ferric ammonium citrate
    Elixar of Vitrol — elixir of vitriol — aromatic sulphuric acid
    columbo — as 34
    decolion bark — not known
    cascarilla — bitter from the bark of a tree, croton eleuteria
    the comment under 20 for sulphuric acid applies here also
41 One is taxed to attempt a translation of 3 pennyworth into todays values
42 spermaceti — fatty material extracted from the head of the Sperm Whale
43 ervalanta — the ervum lens, not the common lentil
44 saltpetre — crude sodium aitrate
45 only a qualified chiropodist should 'pare' a corn
46 assumed to mean spirits of wine
47 it is very dangerous to interfere with moles in any way
48 turkey rhubarb — Rheum palmatum, one of the edible rhubarbs —
    laxative
    guaicum — the resin of guaiacum wood
    £500 in those days was a considerable sum, if the tale be true

49   cantharides — dried spanish fly
50   this has a note in the original, 'from Mr. Howitt, Heanor by Dr. G. B. Norman'
      cascarilla bark — see 40
51   german yeast — not known
      the original has a footnote, 'Mrs. Upton'
52   sulphuric ether — see 21
      gum mastic — similar to gamboge, see 14
53   sassafras oil — from the bark of a North American tree
54   this has a footnote, 'Dr. Forbes, Eastwood, Notts'.
55   bold but innacurate claims
56   if only it were that simple
57   foxglove contains digitalis, a poison
58   Always a good seller, but men as always, still go bald
59   elixir of vitriol — see
      another 'sure cure'. A footnote states, 'Cleethorpes 1901'
60   no units are given for 'peel', ozs can be assumed
61   bichromatic potash — potassium bichromate
      germain — german silver, an alloy of nickel, zinc and copper
62   ind meal — indian meal or maize
63   the only references to the resale value of any of the recipes
64   cream (of) tartar is potassium acid tartrate
65   carrander — coriander, plant with aromatic fruit, used for flavouring soups etc.
66   galls — the oak gall contains tannin
      green vitriol — Iron Sulphate
      logwood — a dye from heamatoxylum campechianum
67   nothing that is available domestically should be applied to burns, scolds, etc.
68   opodolese — liniment of soap (opodeldoc)
      cajeput oil — cajuput oil — oil from leaves and twigs from a species of melaleuca
      cantharides — see 49
69   cerate — rose water
70   orris — from the root of the iris
      cardemon — see 19
71   sperm oil — from the Sperm Whale
72   copperas — Iron sulphate, green vitriol
      logwood — see 66
      galls — see 66

73 no units for the peel again. A footnote says 'Mrs. Jackson'

74 footnote as 73, the writer's mother?

75 a footnote says, 'These two are made by a Baker'
    no units for the peel

76 a word must be missing from here, 'properly'!
    a footnote says 'Professor P. A. Simpson, M.D.'

77 bacillicon — a type of ointment that is a 'sovereign' remedy

78 blood root — see 12
    wine of antimony — see 29
    tolu — see 28
    squill — see 28
    ipecae — assumed to be an abbreviation of ipecacuanha, see 23
    paregoric — see 28
    gum mucilage arabic — gum arabic, exudate from acacia senegal
    a footnote says 'T. Jackson', a reference to the writer?

79 bark of bittersweet — woody nightshade (solanum dulcaniara)
    tumors — not as we understand them today

80 yellow wax — beeswax
    burgundy pitch — see 39
    venice turpentine — oleoresin of larch

81 see 67

82 verdigris — green crystals formed by the action of acetic acid on copper

83 see 67 above, the use of white or red lead is not recommended and could
    be illegal

84 spermaceti — see 42 above

85 sal ammoniac — ammonium chloride

86 white ether — same as 20 and 21 above

87 arrow root — a nutritious starch

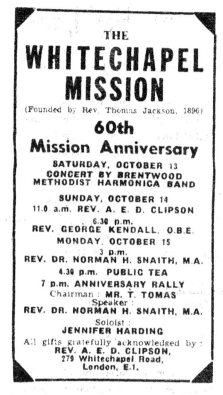

THE

WHITECHAPEL MISSION

(Founded by Rev. Thomas Jackson, 1896)

60th
Mission Anniversary

SATURDAY, OCTOBER 13
CONCERT BY BRENTWOOD
METHODIST HARMONICA BAND

SUNDAY, OCTOBER 14
11.0 a.m. REV. A. E. D. CLIPSON
6.30 p.m.
REV. GEORGE KENDALL, O.B.E.

MONDAY, OCTOBER 15
3 p.m.
REV. DR. NORMAN H. SNAITH, M.A.

4.30 p.m. PUBLIC TEA

7 p.m. ANNIVERSARY RALLY
Chairman : MR. T. TOMAS
Speaker :
REV. DR. NORMAN H. SNAITH, M.A.

Soloist :
JENNIFER HARDING

All gifts gratefully acknowledged by :
REV. A. E. D. CLIPSON,
279 Whitechapel Road,
London, E.1.

Reprinted from The Methodist Recorder, October 11th, 1956.

Grandfather Thomas Jackson, followed in his uncle's footsteps. Thomas Jackson the elder, founded the still thriving Whitechapel Mission in 1896. He was born in Belper in October 1850 and died some 80 years later.

The publishers are indebted to the Revd. Peter Jennings of the Mission for this information.

John Merrill's -
"My Derbyshire" Historical Series.

A TO Z GUIDE TO THE PEAK DISTRICT by John N. Merrill
WINSTER - A SOUVENIR GUIDE .by John N. Merrill
DERBYSHIRE INNS - an A TO Z GUIDE . by John N. Merrill
HALLS & CASTLES OF THE PEAK DISTRICT. by John N. Merrill.
DERBYSHIRE FACTS AND RECORDS by John N. Merrill
THE STORY OF THE EYAM PLAGUE by Claence Daniel
THE EYAM DISCOVERY TRAIL by Clarence Daniel
PEAK DISTRICT SKETCHBOOK by John N. Merrill
LOST DERBYSHIRE VILLAGE WALKS - VOL 1 & 2 by John N. Merrill
TOURING THE PEAK DISTRICY & DERBYSHIRE BY CAR by John N. Merrill
LOST INDUSTRIES OF DERBYSHIRE by John N. Merrill
DESERTED MEDIEVAL VILLAGES OF DERBYSHIRE by John N. Merrill

FAMOUS DERBYSHIRE PEOPLE -
ARKWRIGHT OF CROMFORD by John N. Merrill.
SIR JOSEPH PAXTON by John N. Merrill
FLORENCE NIGHTINGALE by John N. Merrill
JOHN SMEDLEY by John N. Merrill
MARY QUEEN OF SCOTS - "The Captive Queen." by John N. Merrill
BESS OF HARDWICK - "The Costly Countess" by John N. Merrill
THE EARLS AND DUKES OF DEVONSHIRE by John N. Merrill

GHOSTS & LEGENDS -
DERBYSHIRE FOLKLORE.by John N. Merrill.
DERBYSHIRE PUNISHMENT by John N. Merrill.
CUSTOMS OF THE PEAK DISTRICT & DERBYS by John N. Merrill
LEGENDS OF DERBYSHIRE. by John N. Merrill.
GRANDFATHER THOMAS JACKSON'S VICTORIAN CURES & RECIPES

PEAK DISTRICT VISITOR'S GUIDES by John N. Merrill
ASHOURNE   BAKEWELL   MATLOCK

DERBYSHIRE HISTORY THROUGH THE AGES -
Vol 1 - DERBYSHIRE IN PREHISTORIC TIMES by John N. Merrill
Vol 3 - DERBYSHIRE IN NORMAN TIMES by John N. Merrill